HOPSCOTCH
MYTHS

# Icarus,
## the Boy Who Flew

by Barrie Wade and David Lopez

W
FRANKLIN WATTS
LONDON•SYDNEY

Long ago Icarus lived
with his father, Daedalus.
Daedalus was a great inventor.

5

One day the king asked Daedalus to build him a giant maze. It was to hide a terrible secret.

So Daedalus built the biggest maze anyone had ever seen.

The king was delighted. But he locked Daedalus and Icarus in a prison tower. They knew the king's secret, so they could never leave.

Birds came to eat the crumbs that
Icarus left by the window. Then, as
the birds flew away, a few feathers
floated down.

"I wish I was as free as a bird,"
Icarus said sadly. Daedalus smiled.
"I have a plan," he said.

"Help me collect these feathers
until we have enough to fly!"
Daedulus said. So Icarus found
as many as he could.

Daedalus worked for many
months. He tied the feathers
together with thread. Then he
stuck them down with candle wax.

At last, Daedalus finished. He had made two huge pairs of wings.

"Let's go now!" cried Icarus.

He longed to fly out of the tower.

"All right, my son," said his father. "But remember not to fly too low, or the sea spray will make your wings wet and heavy.

"Don't fly too high either,
or the sun will melt them."
"Yes Father," said Icarus, but
he wasn't really listening.

Iacrus longed to fly like a bird.
He went up to the window and
jumped out, with Daedalus close
behind him.

Icarus flapped his wings – he could fly! He felt the rush of air as he flew. "I'm free!" he shouted.

He could glide ...

and he could dive!

"Icarus! Not too low!" his father
shouted. Icarus remembered the
sea spray and flapped his wings.

He climbed in circles, higher and higher into the light. This was even better than diving!

Daedalus was shouting below but
Icarus was too high to hear him.

Higher and higher soared Icarus, dizzy with excitement.

Then he remembered the sun –
but it was too late!

The wax was already melting.

Feathers began to fall off.

Icarus dived down to cooler air.
His feathers fell away like flower
petals. Down and down he fell.

Like a stone he dropped into the sea. His father watched helplessly.

For a moment a few feathers
floated like foam on the water,
then sank. Icarus was lost forever.

Daedalus threw his wings away.

He never flew again.

Hopscotch has been specially designed to fit the requirements of the Literacy Framework. It offers real books by top authors and illustrators for children developing their reading skills. There are 63 Hopscotch stories to choose from:

* **hardback**